Puppy Poems

Gaby Morgan is Editorial Director of the Macmillan Children's Books poetry list. She has edited a number of bestselling anthologies, including *Read Me: A Poem for Every Day of the Year*, *Christmas Poems* and *In My Sky at Twilight*. *Fairy Poems* was shortlisted for the 2007 CLPE Poetry Award. She lives in Hampshire with Grant, Jude and Evie.

Jane Eccles lives in Hampshire with Graham and Theo. She loves dogs and cats and longs for a whippet or a retired greyhound.

Puppy Poems

Chosen by Gaby Morgan

Illustrated by Jane Eccles

MACMILLAN CHILDREN'S BOOKS

For Taliesin, 1973–1984 – a mighty fine dog –
and for my wonderful godmother Madeleine Brunt,
who knew that a small girl needed a dog by her side.
And for all the other Morgan dogs: Lucy, Mo, Jack, Amy,
Saffy, Eddie, Ruby and Lila – GM

For Maddie and for Sophie with love from Jane

First published 2011 by Macmillan Children's Books
a division of Macmillan Publishers Limited
20 New Wharf Road, London N1 9RR
Basingstoke and Oxford
Associated companies throughout the world
www.panmacmillan.com

ISBN 978-0-330-52770-5

1 3 5 7 9 8 6 4 2

A CIP catalogue record for this book is available from
the British Library.

Printed and bound in the UK by CPI Mackays, Chatham ME5 8TD

Contents

Dream Puppy

I've got a dream puppy I call Scruff.
She's a bouncing, pouncing ball of fluff
who will chase a stick or sit and stay.
She's in my daydreams every day.
When I'm at school, dream puppy's there
snoozing underneath my chair
and in my dreams at night I see
her little figure following me.
One day, dream puppy, you'll come true.
Till then I'll wait. I'll wait for you.

Marian Swinger

Puppy

Squeaky yapper,
Fluffy snapper.

Wobbly walker,
Bug stalker.

Shoe chewer,
Clothes strewer.

Fly catcher,
Ear scratcher.

Paper ripper,
Teacup tipper.

Tail chaser,
Chaos maker.

Food guzzler,
Big-eyed nuzzler.

Tired cutie,
Sleeping beauty . . .

Kevin McCann

2

Message to K9

K9, you were my hero
though you were made of tin.
I loved your flashing eyes
and the way your ears could spin.

Now you've left the Doctor,
would you like to live with me?
I'd oil your joints and polish you.
Please say that you agree,

for we could go adventuring
if only you were mine.
We'd travel through the universe,
just you and me, K9.

Marian Swinger

Hello Puppy

A single shining star
In a pale blue early evening sky
Darkness like the tide
Sweeping through the universe
Washing away the light
As we trampoline down
The bumpy muddy track

Farmyard lights burn like beacons
A lighthouse in the hillside
Beating back the encroaching
Cold winter evening

The puppies were playing
With a punctured football
In the twilight of the day
Scampering across the yard
Whilst the cows in the barn
Watched with emotionless eyes

'Do you know why
we're here?'
I asked my son

Joseph's face lit up
Like a Christmas tree

'To get a dog' he replied

And the bell began to ring
And the choirs began to sing
In a fairy-tale fantasy
But in the farmyard of reality
My son was playing with the puppies
Who were playing with a ball
Having a ball
In the dusk of the day

'Our dog' was playing
With our son.

Tony Bower

Puppy Dreaming

On the nylon hearthrug,
Whippy tail flicking,
One tooth bared,
A sleeping puppy dreams:

Along well-worn deer trails
He's running,
A swerving swift grey shadow
Who keeps up easily
With the pack
Reflected in his new-leaf eyes,
Paws kicking back
Silver crumbs
As pad and claw skim a crust of ice
Until he scrambles a snowy mound
Where bare rock flexes up
Through moonstruck white,
Sits back on iron haunches
Singing in the night:

And on the nylon hearthrug,
Whippy tail flicking,
One tooth bared,
A sleeping puppy dreams.

Kevin McCann

Joys of Spring

When sparkling showers
shine on spring flowers,
my dogs and I go strolling.
As my heart sings,
they find dead things
to sniff, and chew, and roll in.

Jane Clarke

The Animal Shelter

Today we went to the Animal Shelter
because we're all agreed we'd like
a puppy.
We've promised
we'll walk him
and talk to him,
brush him
and we'll love him oh so much.

We went past the kennels
to the puppy pens
and all the dogs begged us
to walk them
and talk to them,
play every day with them,
brush them
and love them oh so much –

and in the very last kennel
was a little terrier.

She didn't wag her tail
nor bark, nor beg us to take her home
and walk her . . .

but talk to her
and stay with her
and love her oh so much.

She just sat there,
sad.

Then she came up to us.

And we all looked at each other.

We never got as far as the puppy pens.

We call her Lucky
and we love her oh so much.

Judith Green

Pet Passport

one wagger
one licker
one sniffer
two lookers

two flappers
four shifters
eighteen scratchers
forty-two snappers

Mike Johnson

Night Patrol

Before we settle down to sleep
It's my job to check the four corners
Of the garden

Behind the bins for lurking rats

Search the long shed shadows
Lest the Beast of Midnight is waiting there

Check the pond for late-night hoppers

Patrol the fence for creeping cats

All is well and I have a warm feeling
Knowing my human
Can sleep safely at night

Roger Stevens

Dog Dreaming

Lying on the rug and dozing
– Rabbit dreams . . .
Supposing that I'm nosing
Into burrows on the high hill,
Up above the furrows
Of the black ploughed fields.
There's wolf in me,
All the cunning of the pack
Runs in my blood
And rises in the hair along my back.

Lying on the rug and dozing
– Closing half an eye . . .
Returning with a shuddering sigh
To the wild woods – wild ways.
Old, old days before you drew us in
And tamed us, claimed us,
Collared us and named us.
Gave us everything we wanted,
Took from us everything we had.
Only now, in the deep, deep sleep,
My heart remembers how it was
And hunts.

Jan Dean

Who's Going to
Walk the Dog?

'Who's going to walk the dog?'

'Oh *what*?'
'It's raining!'
'You must be joking!'
'I've got homework.'
'Washing-up.'
'Music practice.'

'You can walk the dog first.'

'But I did it yesterday!'
'I did it the day before.'
'I did it last week.'
'I did it in the holidays.'

Huffing and puffing, Mum takes the lead,
shrugs on her dog-walking coat,

pulls on her dog-walking hat,
shoves her feet into the mud-spotted boots
which she wore
yesterday . . .
the day before . . .
last week . . .
in the holidays . . .
when SHE walked the dog.

She lets the door slam as she leaves.

Amber licks Mum's hand gratefully,
bounds off joyfully,
chases a ball enthusiastically,
plunges into the water splashily,
shakes her coat out drenchingly,
looks up adoringly.

Mum and Amber race to the top of the hill.
They look out over the rain-streaked valley
and the metal-grey river
and the washed-through trees

and Mum has already forgotten
why she'd asked someone else
to walk the dog.

Anna Wilson

Jack

Jack
is my best friend,
I know I can trust him.
I don't have to win things
or prove that I'm strong.
When I'm in trouble
and nobody likes me,
I just call for Jack –
he's for *me*, right or wrong.

Jack
is my best friend,
who shares all my secrets.
My partner for ball games
and jumping off beds.
The last one I see
as I drift into sleep,
and just as the pictures
of night fill my head . . .

Jack licks my nose.

Daphne Kitching

Royal Dogs

They ride in chauffeured limousines
and private planes. They are the Queen's,
for even queens need someone that
they can take for walks and pat,
someone furry, fun and sweet,
who'll sit beside the royal feet.
Where else would anybody royal
find a friend so true and loyal?

Marian Swinger

View from a Small Bridge

As the water flows under
I feel it somehow lifting
into the blue sky
below me above.

My lurcher
comes wandering back.
Looking up at me.
Looking into the water.
Sensing distance.

Des Dillon

Judy Dog's School Report

Barking: Excellent.
Very loud
Especially in car when she sees another dog.
Makes Mum jump.
And swerve.

Sense of Smell: Excellent.
Can sniff out dead hedgehogs and foxes' poo
From half a mile away.

Being Told to Sit: Room for improvement.
Has to be told twice.

Guard Duty: Could do better.
She greets strangers with a wagging tail
And tries to bite the postwoman.

Companionship: Excellent.
Always there when you're feeling low.
Always pleased to see you.
Especially at mealtimes.

Roger Stevens

Flint

Flint is as meek as a mouse but as brave as a
   lion
He is as small as the hole he likes to climb
   in.

Flint is as white as the snow but spotted
   with dirt
He is as round as a ball but as slim as a
   spear.

Flint is as hungry as the wolf but as sleepy
   as a sloth
He is happy to kiss and lovely to hold.

Flint is as slow as a clock but as fast as the
   time
He is a guard dog at night and a kitten by
   day.

Flint is a bear-growling dog and a fish with
    a grin
He will bark very loud and snore every sleep.

Flint is a dog called Jack, but we don't call
    him that
He is my friend all the time and the best in
    the world.

And I love him
because he is mine.

Carol Mead

My Three-Legged Dog

My dog has three legs.
People say, 'Ah,' 'shame,' or just look away.
But he's very happy and does all sorts of dog
  things.
He even wins the three-legged race every
  Sports Day.

He sniffs with other dogs,
Wags with other dogs,
Barks with other dogs,
Plays chase with other dogs.

The four-legged dogs don't seem to notice.
The four-legged dogs don't walk away.

Humans could learn a lot from dogs.

Tim Pointon

The Things a Dog Has to Do

Clean the kitchen floor lest tiny scraps of
  food should spoil the appearance of the
  tiles.
Listen to the wind to mark a change in the
  weather.
Watch carefully the cat, lest her nerve breaks
  and she makes a dash for the window.

Guard the window lest the poodle over the
  road uses insulting barking.
Remind potential burglars that she would
  make a fearsome adversary.
Check, by sniffing, that other dogs have
  clean bottoms.

Check, by sniffing, the four corners of the house for intruders.

Check, also by sniffing, the four corners of the garden for the same.

Seek the remnants of dead hedgehogs or other small animals and mark by rolling in them.

Watch the toy bone lest it move of its own accord.

Remind her owner, by subtle means, that it is time for a walk.

Remind her owner by less-subtle means that it is time to eat.

Bark loudly for no reason – just for the sheer hell of it and to keep owner on toes.

Puzzle over unusual configurations of
   clouds.
Guard the front door lest the postman breaks
   in to steal a letter.
Wonder why the strange man who gave
   her the tasty bone is coming through the
   window and not the door.

Roger Stevens

At the Seaside

My puppy's never seen the sea
before, he look at me and barks –
this rolling mass that rushes in,
it isn't there in parks.

It chases him then runs away,
he cannot understand,
his feet are wet, he licks the spray –
it's a strange and salty land.

Judith Green

31

I'm a Border Collie

I'm a young Border collie, a charmer,
And I'm learning to work with the farmer.
 When his whistle goes 'Peeeeep'
 I should round up his sheep –
If I don't, there's a big melodrama!

Pam Gidney

I'm a Springer Spaniel

My colouring's white mixed with liver,
And I love spending time in the river.
 But I work hard as well –
 I can track things by smell:
Smuggled goods, roadside bombs – I'll
 deliver!

Pam Gidney

Hot Pavement

hot pavement –
my dog's shadow
under mine

Liz Brownlee

The Wizard's Dog

The wizard's dog
doesn't bury bones.
He hides stars.

He doesn't go walkies.
He flies.

He doesn't fetch sticks.
He brings back wands.

But he does chase
the witch's cat.

And when his master gets home
he goes crazy
with excitement and love.

So, in many ways,
he is a fairly ordinary
sort of dog.

The wizard's dog.

Bernard Young

Stick

It might seem obvious to you humans
But it puzzles me every day
If he wants the stick so badly
Why does he throw it away?

Roger Stevens

Over Here

We are over here
Our dog is   over there

We wish our dog
Was over here,
    but our dog is   over there

We've been calling our dog
To come over here,
    but she's still   over there

Our dog is still   over there

Over where the seagulls are escaping
And flying, flying through the air

Tony Bower

I Do As Simon Says

I'm nobody's dog but Simon's
I do as Simon says,
If Simon said, 'Delilah, dance!'
I'd be up on my two hind legs.

But Simon says, 'Delilah, sit!'
He says, 'Delilah, stay!'
Yet if he said, 'Delilah, sing!'
I'd somehow find a way.

I'm nobody's dog but Simon's
I do as Simon says,
He sometimes says, 'Delilah, fetch!'
And I save Simon's legs.

But Simon is no tyrant,
He takes me out for walks,
I always keep one step ahead
And listen as he talks.

My watchword is Obedience,
And Simon's love my prize,
We go together everywhere
For I am Simon's eyes.

Celia Warren

In the Corn

in the corn
ears appear, disappear
a puppy jumps

Liz Brownlee

The Blind Dog

My kindly human sighs for me,
But with my clever nose I see . . .

The perfumed path of a lady dog,
The fishy trail of a passing frog,

The sharp, clear stink of a scavenging fox,
The tempting scents of a cardboard box,
The glorious odours of dustbin day,
The tang of a lamp post in my way,

The feathery whiff of a broken bird,
The traces of ice cream, softly blurred,

The insults left by an old tomcat,
The slimy tracks of a sewer rat,
The homely smell of our garden gate,
The call of the gravy on my plate.

My kindly human sighs for me,
But with my clever nose – I see.

Clare Bevan

The Fur Alarm Clock

The fur alarm clock
Licks my face
As it will tomorrow
And did yesterday.
And the pay-off
Is brown biscuits
Ice-cold water
In a silver bowl.
And then a stroll.
He's dragging me
Upon my lead.
So on we go
Both panting hard
From running madly
On the shore.

Faster and faster
Barney bounds
And bounds
And barks.
The seagulls scatter.
The sea is gleaming after rain.
Life is so good
For a boy and dog
Together again.

David Clayton

My Dog

I love my dog.
My dog loves me.
Wherever I go
So does he.

Whatever I do
He does too.
He stays close by me
All day through.

He makes me happy
When I feel sad.
He even likes me
When I've been bad,

And when I'm grumpy
He doesn't mind.
He's always gentle,
Warm and kind.

He's my best friend –
Anyone can see.
I love my dog.
My dog loves me.

Gillian Floyd

The Dark Avenger

My dog is called The Dark Avenger
Hello, I'm Cuddles

She understands every word I say
Woof?

Last night I took her for a walk
Woof! Walkies! Let's go!

Cleverly, she kept three paces ahead
I dragged him along behind me

She paused at every danger, spying out the
    land
I stopped at every lamp post

When the coast was clear, she sped on
I slipped my lead and ran away

Scenting danger, Avenger investigated
I found some fresh chip papers in the bushes

I followed, every sense alert
He blundered through the trees, shouting,
'Oy, come 'ere! Where are you?'

Something – maybe a sixth sense – told me
   to stop
He tripped over me in the dark

There was a pale menacing figure ahead of
   us
Then I saw the white Scottie from next door

Avenger sprang into battle, eager to defend
   her master
Never could stand terriers

They fought like tigers
We scrapped like dogs

Until the enemy was defeated
Till Scottie's owner pulled him off –
   spoilsport!

Avenger gave a victory salute
I rolled in the puddles

And came to check I was all right
I shook mud over him

'Stop it, you stupid dog!'
He congratulated me

Sometimes, even The Dark Avenger can go
   too far.
Woof!! Woof!! Yelp . . . !

Trevor Millum

My Dog Smells

My dog smells
The faint scent of
Cats to chase.

Her nose twinkles
Like a black star,
When it's chicken
On Sunday.

She reads the garden
Breeze like a child
With a first comic.
Empty-looking air
Is full of information,
Messages incoming as
She fills her lungs.

And when, in the woods,
She finds where
Foxes have been,
She rolls, and then . . .
. . . my dog smells!

Robin Mellor

The Ballad of Beddgelert

Prince Llywelyn owned a faithful hound,
    And Gelert was his name.
Seven hundred years ago in Wales
    He earned immortal fame.

One day, when Llywelyn blew his horn
    To summon all his pack,
Gelert, the leader, failed to come,
    But when the prince came back

From his day's hunt, his dog ran up!
    His jaws with blood were red.
The prince thought, Has he killed my child?
    Ran to the infant's bed.

He found the cradle overturned,
    Blood on the sheets and wall,
But of his tender little child
    There was no sign at all.

Then, mad with grief, he plunged his sword
    Straight into Gelert's side,
And at that moment, faint yet clear,
    The prince's baby cried!

He found his son beneath his cot,
    Unharmed, and in no pain!
Next to him lay a fearsome wolf
    Whom brave Gelert had slain!

Filled with remorse, the prince, distraught,
    Picked up his faithful hound,
Carried him out beyond the gates
    And raised to him a mound,

A cairn of stones to mark the place
    Where valiant Gelert lay,
And Gelert's grave, or 'Beddgelert',
    Can still be seen today.

Pam Gidney

My Invisible Dog

My invisible dog
Is not much fun.
I can't tell when
He's glad or glum.

I can't tell if
When I pat his head
I'm really patting
His bum instead.

Brian Patten

Who's the Retriever?

Our dog's meant to be a retriever,
But when we throw her ball,
She flops down on the grass
And shows no interest at all.

But if she sees a cat,
She jumps up with a bark
And we have to retrieve her
By chasing her round the park!

John Foster

Sam's Song

My favourite walk
is across the fields –
we leave behind the stupid sheep
with their wonderful stink
and their *bleat, bleat, bleat,*
then my human stops
and unfastens my lead . . .

I race to the river, shallow
and clear, stony and wide,
and I take a run
as it's surely alive!

I stand on the stones,
snap at the water
trying to catch it
but just as I caught
a great bite of it – *Woof!*
and I'm barking . . .

Woof! Woof! I go, barking
Woof! Woof! in the water
(occasional *Snap!* at it!)
Woof! I go
   heartily
     loving
     the barking . . .
   my whole body thrills to it.
Somewhere a faint calling –
my human is yelling
but all I know *Woof! Woof!* is water
and *Woof! Woof!*
I'm *Woof! Woof! Woof!*
   loving it
     loving this
     Woof! Woof! Woof!
     barking.

Joan Poulson

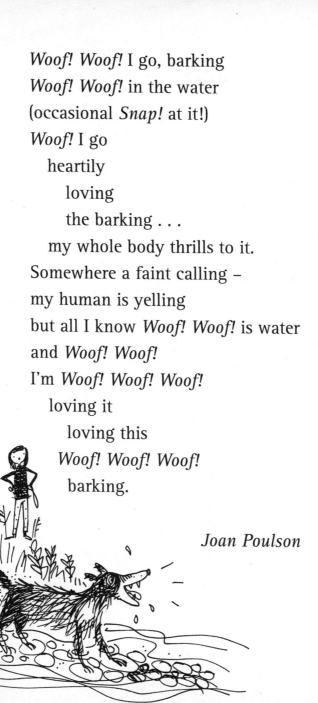

Walkies

Dog years tick tock tick quicker
than human years, they say,

so please excuse me if I pant
and take my time today:

it's not my fault. I *ran*
before you walked or learned to play.

By the time you started school,
I was turning slightly grey.

Blame nature and not me
if I'm past doggy middle age;

my book's nearing the end,
you're still on the second page.

Let me sniff a little longer,
shuffling through leaves –

autumn is my favourite time . . .
soon spring's blooms you'll breathe:

think of me as you walk here then,
our marvellous memories;

all that fun together, chasing,
running round these trees!

Yes, there's a reason why I'll pant
and take my time today:

dog years tick tock tick quicker
than human years, they say.

Mike Johnson

The Three Dogs

There are three little dogs
In Mrs Brown's house –
Froo-Froo and Bonzo and me.
Froo-Froo wins trophies,
And Bonzo's a star,
But I sleep on Mrs Brown's knee.

Froo-Froo is cute
From the tip of her tail
To the ribbon on top of her head.
Bonzo's an actor
On children's TV,
But I sleep on Mrs Brown's bed.

Froo-Froo is fluffy,
She struts down
     the street
With her elegant
     nose in the air.
Bonzo's a hero,
An athlete, a clown,
But I sleep on Mrs Brown's chair.

There are three little dogs
In Mrs Brown's house –
Froo-Froo and Bonzo and me.
Froo-Froo likes prizes,
And Bonzo loves fame . . .
But I prefer Mrs Brown's knee.

Clare Bevan

In Holiday Mood

I'm in such a good mood today.
My master is going away!

He'll take me to his brother Ted,
Who lets me sleep upon the bed,

Who always takes me in the car,
Even when they're not going far,

Who gives me snacks between my meals,
Who really knows how a dog feels,

Who lets me chase across the park,
And doesn't mind it when I bark,

Who comes to open the back door,
As soon as I scratch with my paw,

Who lets me sprawl upon the chairs,
And doesn't mind if I leave hairs,

Who praises me for being so good,
And treats me as a human should.

I'm in such a good mood today.
My master's off on holiday.

John Foster

Petronius Pertinax Parvus the Third

(It is said that the Romans owned the smallest dogs in the world, so PERHAPS this tale is true.)

I swear by the Gods, and I give you my
    word –
Petronius Pertinax Parvus the Third

Was the littlest dog in
    all of the land!
He gnawed on a mouse-
    bone; he sat in my hand;

His lead was a ribbon of spidery
    thread;
He raced across tables; he rode on my head;

He slept in a snail shell; he chased after
    fleas;

He guarded me
   bravely from
   wasps and from
   bees;

His snarl was as soft as the fall of a pin,
But his bite could draw blood from a kitchen
   rat's skin.

He'd beg for a crumb, or a game with a twig;
His body was small, yet his heart was so big

No friend could be greater, I give you my
   word,
Than Petronius Pertinax Parvus the Third.

Clare Bevan

*PS 'Pertinax' means 'Steadfast',
and 'Parvus' means 'Small'.*

The Tale of the Dog

'Man's Best Friend' –
That's what they call me;
And that's what I BELIEVED –
Until THE CAT arrived!

Whereas I have to be
'Faithful and obedient',
SIT when ordered,
Fetch ANY ball or stick,
GROWL at unwelcome callers,
NEVER stay out at night –
And stand on my hind legs
For a few MISERABLE chocolate drops . . .

THE CAT (on the other hand)
Can 'lounge around',
Preen herself FOR HOURS,
Slink away disdainfully
Whenever visitors arrive,
And SCRATCH to pieces

ANYONE who strokes her
When she wants to go to sleep.
She can STAY AWAY
For NIGHTS ON END –
And always get
A WARM WELCOME
When she returns!

It's none of the
'SIT! STAY! BAD DOG!'
Kind of talk
They keep dishing out to ME –
And yet she STILL gets fed
AND sheltered!

'Man's Best Friend', eh?
It looks like
I shall have to do some
SERIOUS RETHINKING
About THAT!

Trevor Harvey

Retriever

Our dog Goldie is a retriever.
Dad says Goldie's family,
her mother and father,
her grandparents, great-grandparents –
even her great-great-great-grandparents,
were all carefully selected and bred
to give Goldie her extraordinary skill at
retrieving sticks . . .
Seems a bit far-fetched to me.

Philip Waddell

Sunday Walking

Sunday walking,
laughing, talking,
wind blowing,
cheeks glowing,
leaves flying,
seagulls crying,
clouds racing,
dog chasing,
ball rolling,
people strolling,
sun setting,
cold getting,
homeward scurrying,
shivering, hurrying,
front door closing,
people dozing,
coal fire roaring,
dog snoring.

Geraldine Aldridge

Sheepdog

There are no roads where I work
On the open Dales,
I go whatever the weather,
Sun, rain or roaring gales.

My master just whistles
To tell me what to do,
I gently circle, rounding up
Every lamb and every ewe.

When it's time to settle
This is my spot on the grass,
It's good to stretch my paws out,
Get some rest at last.

But I'm ready in a moment,
I don't mind the work at all,
I'm off, at the run, to my master;
I hear his call.

Robin Mellor

Walking the Dog

When Dad and I took our dog for a walk . . .

She chased a fat cat over a log,
she barked and barked at a jumping frog.

She opened her mouth and caught a fly,
she lay on her back and stared at the sky.

She licked my ice cream when I wasn't
     looking,
she sniffed the smell of pies that were
     cooking.

She wanted to come on the slide with us,
she howled and made such a terrible fuss.

Then she rolled in something that smelt
     really bad,
so I walked ahead and left her with Dad.

And after our walk, which had taken an
     hour . . .

Our dog had a bath . . .

And then gave us a shower!

                    Brian Moses

Our Dog Is Special

Our dog is unique.
He is no known breed.
But that our dog is special
We are all agreed.

He'll sit when you tell him.
He's alert and on guard.
He barks when a stranger
Comes into our yard.

When I come home from school
He is lying in wait
To jump up and greet me
When I come through the gate.

Then he fetches his lead
Which hangs in the hall
And we go on a search
For his favourite ball.

Then it's off to the park
Where he scampers about
And we stay there and play there
Until he's worn out.

At night he curls up
With his head on my knee
And I ruffle his fur
While I'm watching TV.

Our dog is unique.
He has no pedigree
But that our dog is special
We all agree.

John Foster

Blossom, the Emperor's Noble Dog
(for Shar Peis everywhere)

Blossom's stately head,
Wrinkled and crinkled
Like the map of a mountain,
Lifts from her dreams.

Her gaze is solemn,
With ancient wisdom
She solves vast problems
Of weighty mathematics,
Puzzles of Time
And the faraway stars.

Adored by Emperors,
When she trotted past
Imperial Guards roared their devotion,
Servants and courtiers in flowing robes
Bowed low in her honour,

Huge Dragon Gates of intricate iron
Swung open, she gave a soft bark
And the Empress smiled.

Blossom sleeps once more,
Dreams of chasing the civet
And the jade-green serpents
With golden tongues
Over endless plains
Towards the sun-reddened horizon.

Then wakes and smiles,
Guarding her deep-as-the-ocean
Secrets forever.

David Harmer

The Princess's Treasure

The Princess's dog had eyes as sharp as
   spindles
And a tail that wagged like a royal flag.

By night he guarded her door as fiercely as a
   dragon
Even though he was no bigger
Than a dungeon rat.
And he feared no one,
Not even the palace soldiers
In their clumping iron boots.

The Princess called him Treasure.
She smoothed his bristly coat
With a mermaid's lost comb,
And whenever she visited the Wide World
He sat beside her in the royal carriage.

His glossy nose could sniff, sniff, sniff
The one true Prince
In a crowd of thousands,
And he was never once fooled
By a tattered coat
Or a broken wooden sword.

Clare Bevan

Storm

He scrambles into my bed.
There's a storm.
I bury my nose in his fur.
He smells warm.
He quivers and shakes
with each lightning flash.
He shivers and quakes
with each thunderous crash.
I snuggle him up to me,
cuddle him near.
With terrified whimper
he nuzzles my ear.
Now the storm has passed
and the garden is steaming,
he's peaceful at last,
silently dreaming.

Geraldine Aldridge

Old Dog

The cats don't worry any more
word's out; five minutes' walk
from bed to chair. This year
fireworks weren't pain. You
didn't even seem to hear. Dull-
eyed, head buried in my lap, you
lift my hand dry-nosed, and I
caress the grey straw of your fur

You were never beautiful or good,
a raggle-taggle mischief of a dog,
but that was long ago . . . Now
in your dreams you run and play.
And we who cursed half-eaten shoes
smile as you sniff secret smells
in a doggy heaven we can't share

Sue Hardy-Dawson

Street Dogs

Terrier Tom lives at No. 14,
Only one eye and a stump of a tail.
Roars down our street like a
   bad-tempered wind,
Dines on pork pie
   and a saucer of ale.

Cherry Pie Champ is the pride
   of the Joneses,
Gleaming white coat and a collar of blue.
Stares from the window at soft-stepping
   cats,
Pampered and bored,
   with nothing to
   do.

Scamp's called 'the
   happy dog', fat
   and content,

Lies on the back
    wall, basks in
    the sun,
Sits by the lamp post
    and *smiles* all the day,
Never moves far from his home, No.1.

But **Wilfred**'s our school dog, brown as a
    wolf,
Rough-haired and lanky, with eyes glinting
    green.
Begs for Maltesers, cheese sarnies and crisps,
'Stands up for Jesus', and 'dies for the
    Queen'.

Graeme Curry

Goodbye, Good Boy

Old, old friend.
Stiff-boned now,
Like Grandma's fingers.
My first true love.
I bury my face in your fur,
Black now streaked with white.
You smell of sunshine
And golden days of play.
You manage to lift your head
And look at me with trusting
Amber eyes.

I recall your puppy days
And all we've shared together since.
The secrets that I've told you,
Best dog. Best friend.
A part of me forever.
Kind hands lift you from me.
It is time.
I will be with you until the end, boy.

I'm right here at your side.
And afterwards? You will live on
In my thoughts,
The happiest wet-nosed memory of all.

But first the pain.
Who knew unhappiness
Could feel like this?
You thump your tail on the
Stainless-steel table.
My heart-bursting wish,
Through burning eyes,
To turn back time.
Goodbye, good boy.
Good dog.

Philip Ardagh

Burying the Dog in the Garden

When we buried
The dog in
The garden on
The grave we put a
Small cross
And the tall
Man next door
Was cross.
'Animals have no
Souls,' he said.
'They must have animal
Souls,' we said.
'No,' he said and
Shook his head.
'Do you need
A soul to
Go to Heaven?' we
Asked. 'Yes,'
He said.

'That means my
Hamster's not
In Heaven,' said
Kevin. 'Nor is
My dog,' I said.
'My cat could sneak
In anywhere,' said
Claire. And we
Thought what a
Strange place
Heaven must be with
Nothing to stroke
For eternity.
Claire was six.
Me and Kevin
Were seven.
We decided we
Did not want
To go to Heaven.
For that the stupid
Man next door
Is to blame.

Brian Patten

Cold Morning

Someone was sweeping a dusting of snow.

From the front door my dog appeared,
    suddenly,
her eyes fixed on mine, her tail a joyous flag
as she galloped and galloped to meet me.
I shrieked her name as she came
and held her gaze long enough to feel her
    soft coat;
rub my head against hers; sense her
    breath . . .
Then I woke.

Dreaming of snow's a good omen, they say.
And to dream of snow in autumn
foreshadows happiness . . .

I'd dream myself an avalanche
if it brought me back my dog.

Celia Warren

A selected list of titles available from Macmillan Children's Books

The prices shown below are correct at the time of going to press. However, Macmillan Publishers reserves the right to show new retail prices on covers, which may differ from those previously advertised.

Read Me and Laugh
Chosen by Gaby Morgan   978-0-330-43557-4   £7.99

Wild! Rhymes That Roar
Chosen by James Carter and
  Graham Denton   978-0-330-46341-6   £4.99

Beware! Low Flying Rabbits
Poems by Roger Stevens   978-0-230-75190-3   £4.99

Greetings, Earthlings!
Space poems by Brian Moses and
  James Carter   978-0-330-47174-9   £4.99

All Pan Macmillan titles can be ordered from our website, www.panmacmillan.com, or from your local bookshop and are also available by post from:

Bookpost, PO Box 29, Douglas, Isle of Man IM99 1BQ

Credit cards accepted. For details:
Telephone: 01624 677237
Fax: 01624 670923
Email: bookshop@enterprise.net
www.bookpost.co.uk

Free postage and packing in the United Kingdom